The Poetry of John Payne

Volume III - The Building of the Dream

John Payne was born on 23rd August 1842 in Bloomsbury, London.

He began his career in the legal profession but thus was soon put to one side as he began his renowned translations of Boccaccio's Decameron, The Arabian Nights, and then the poets Omar Khayyam, François Villon and Diwan Hafez. Of the latter, who he ranked in the same bracket as Dante and Shakepeare, he said; he takes the "whole sweep of human experience and irradiates all things with his sun-gold and his wisdom"

Later Payne became involved with limited edition publishing, and the Villon Society, which was dedicated to the poems of François Villon who was Frances' best known poet of the middle Ages and unfortunately also a thief and a murderer.

John Payne died on 11th February, 1916 at the age of 73 in South Kensington, London.

Index of Contents

THE BUILDING OF THE DREAM

O Love, that never pardoneth,
O Love, more pitiless than Death!
His strife is vain that would express
Thy sweets without thy bitterness.

His toil is vain, for sooth it is
One winneth Love through Death his hiss;
A man shall never know Love's land
Until Death take him by the hand.

O bitter Love! this is indeed
The evil unto life decreed,
That men shall seek thee far and nigh
And finding thee, shall surely die.

I.

There dwelt a squire in Poitou of old times,
Under the fragrant limes
That fringed a city very fair and wide,
Set on a green hill-side;
And all about the city with its slow
Interminable flow.
Faint memories murm'ring of a bygone day,
A river went, that lay
Upon the woven greensward of the fields.
In pools like silver shields
Of fellen giants flung upon the grass,
And round the walls did pass
And kiss'd the grey old ramparts of the place
With the enchanted grace
Of its fair crystal shallows, in the morn
Flushed silver as the thorn
Of a May-dawning and when day was done,
Rose-ruddy with the sun.
That fill'd the arteries of the land with gold.
Fair was the place and old
Beyond the memory of man, with roofs
Tall-peak'd and hung with woofs
Of dainty stone-work, jewell'd with the grace
Of casements, in the face
Of the white gables inlaid, in all hues
Of lovely reds and blues.
At every comer of the winding ways
A carven saint did gaze,
With mild sweet eyes, upon the quiet town.
From niche and shrine of brown;
And many an angel, graven for a charm
To save the folk from harm
Of evil sprites, stood sentinel above
High pinnacle and roof.
The place seem'd sanctified by quietude.
With some quaint peace imbued;
And down its streets the sloping sunlight leant
On roof and battlement,
Like a God's blessing, loath to pass away,
Lingering beyond the day.
But seldom came the pomp and blazonry
Of clamorous war anigh
The calm sweet stead; but there folk came to spend
The days of their life's end

In strifeless quiet, in the tender haze
Of the old knightly days,
That bathed the place in legend and romance.
Haply, bytimes, a lance
Would glitter in the sun, as down the street
The mailed knights rode to meet
The armies of the king of all the land,
And with loud-clanging brand
And noise of many a clarion and a horn,
The bannerets were borne
Before them by their men-at-arms: but yet
The walls were unbeset
By very war and men look'd lazily
Across the plains, to see
The far-off dust-clouds, speck'd with points of light,
That told of coming fight
In the dim distance, where the fighting-men
Trail'd, through some distant glen
Or round the crown of some high-crested hill,
Halberd and spear and bill,
And to the walls the echoed sound would come
Of some great army's hum
And clank of harness, mix'd with trumpet-clang.
And now and then there rang
At the shut gates a silver clarion's call.
And the raised bridge would fall
To give some knight night's harbourage, who went
To a great tournament
Or act of arms in some far distant town
Beyond the purpled brown
Of the great hills. But else the quiet place
Slept in a lazy grace
Of old romance and felt the stress and need
Little in very deed
Of the great world, that compass'd it about
With many a woe and doubt
Unknown to it. Yea, for the quietness
And peace that did possess
The town, had many a learned clerk, that sought
Deep in the mines of thought,
Made to himself a home within the walls;
Among the ancient halls
Wrought many a limner, famous in the land,
And many an one with hand
Well skill'd to sweep the lute-strings to delight,
And crafty men that write
Fair books and fill the marge with painted things,
Gold shapes of queens and kings.

Fair virgins sitting in bird-haunted bowers,
And every weed that flowers
From spring through summer to the waning year,—
Here without let or fear
These all did dwell and wrought at arts of peace.
And there, too, dwelt at ease
This squire of Poitou. Ebhart was his name;
One not unknown to fame
In the old days, when he was wont to rear
Banner and banner'd spear
Before great knights and rend the thickest press
Of foemen with the stress
Of his hot youth. Of old, in very deed.
There once had been much rede
Of his fair prowess and the deeds of arms
He wrought with his stout arms
Upon the enemies of land and king;
And of a truth, no thing
Was wanting to the squire but yet one field
Of fight, ere on his shield
The glorious blazon of a knight should shine.
Before the golden sign
Of chivalry should glance at either heel
And the ennobling steel
Fall softly on his shoulder. But that day
Was long 'since past away
Out of his thought, and all the old desire
Had faded from the squire
Of golden spurs and every knightly thing.
For, as the years did bring
The winterward of life and age began
To creep upon the man.
Came weariness of strife and wish for rest
And thought that peace was best
For those whose youth had left them and the first
Fresh heat of blood, that burst
All bounds and barriers of rugged Fate.
Wherefore he did abate
His warlike toil, and after many a day
He had himself away
From the grim strife and clangour of the time
Wholly withdrawn, in prime
Of later manhood, and in arts of peace
Thenceforward without cease
His mind had vantaged. And in chief, such quests.
As the old alchymists
And nigromancers sought, himself he set
To follow and forget

The ills of living, seeking in old tomes,
Heap'd up within the glooms
Of scholars' shelves for many a dusty year,
To find the words that clear
The secret of the mysteries of life
And all the problems rife
In changeful being, that for aye anew
Unto the sage do sue
For due solution. Many a year he wrought
At these dim quests, and sought—
Chiefest of all the hidden things that lie
And mock men's fantasy
In the recesses of forbidden arts—
The mystic lore that parts
The soul of man from grinding cares of earth
And with a new bright birth
More blessèd than the angels maketh him;
And had upon the brim
Of the strange knowledge trembled many a time.
Yet back into the slime
Of the old state fell ever, missing aye
The thing he did essay
By some hair's-breadth of crystal pitiless.
That against all his stress
Avail'd to stop his passing heavenward.
So, many a year he pour'd
His strength into the sieve of that strange task,
As in a Danald's cask,
And failing ever, ever hoped anew.
And ever did ensue
Upon the well-worn path he loved so well;
Until, one day, it fell
That, studying in an ancient book—fair writ
With chymic inks that bit
Into the pictured vellum of the page
So deeply that with age
The words fail'd scarcely, bound with many a hasp
And quaintly-graven clasp
Of gold and tarnish'd silver,—by some chance
Of favouring Fate, his glance.
That had been wandering dull and listlessly
Amid a prosy sea
Of ancient saws and schoolmen's verbiage,
Lit on a close-writ page.
Whose very aspect made his heart to leap
With some strange stirring. Deep
And long he searched the scroll, till on a space
Left wide betwixt the grace

Of woven flowers and goldwork, that the rim
Of the fair script did limn
With such bright broidery of lovely hues
As ancient folk did use
To beautify their pleasant books withal.
He read a rescript, all
In twisted Greek, contracted to such maze
Of crabbèd Proclus-ways,
That with much labour hardly could he win
To find the sense within
The gnarl'd, rude characters. But well repaid
For all the toil he laid
To the deciphering, in truth, he was;
For so it came to pass
That as the meaning, veil'd at first and dim.
Grew visible to him
More and more certainly, the squire was ware
That in the scroll a rare
And precious secret of the craft lay hid.
Cunningly set amid
A maze of devious words, that, save to one
Long-learn'd and grey-hair'd grown
In all the occult arts, must lead the wit
Wandering astray from it
Among void fancies. But the squire had spent
Long years in study, bent
Over such books, and so was skill'd in all
Devices wherewithal
The ancient masters sought their pearls to hide
From such profane as tried
To fathom their strange mysteries, and keep
Their wisdom dim and deep
For those alone that of the craftship were;
And so, with toil and care.
After much labour from the scroll he learn'd
The thing for which he yearn'd
So many fruitless years; the charm that frees
The soul from miseries
And joys of life: for it therein was told
That, if with virgin gold
Won with his sweat and beaten into shoon.
Beneath the waxing moon.
With his own hands, a man should shoe his horse
And braced for a great coarse,
Should fearless ride into the setting sun,—
Before seven days were done,
He of a truth should come unto a place,
Where, with unearthly grace

And ravishment, the dreams of his dead youth.
In all their lovely sooth
Beyond imagining, should be upbuilt
Before his eyes, and gilt
With all the gold and pearls and flowers that be
Within man's fantasy;
And there it should be given him to dwell
For ever, 'neath the spell
Of that unchanging magic of his thought,
Wherein no thing unsought
For lack of his imagining should fail.
Nor any note of wail
Nor hum of weary toil should enter there.
But in the restful air
Life should be painless under dream-blue skies,
Lit with the radiant eyes
Of that fair queen, whom all in dreams do love.
Set in the realms above
Our reach, as Dante loved his Beatrice.—
And lovelier things than this,
Ay, and more wondrous, were recounted there
Of how that place was fair
And bright beyond man's thought of earthly bliss.
So, little strange it is
If Ebhart, reading of the things set down
Upon the vellum, brown
With age, of that old book, grew wonder-glad
And for a little had
Scarce senses to receive the words he read
And all the goodlihead
Of promise, that the faithful scroll had held
So many a year enspell'd
From all but him the master and adept
Hot tears of joy he wept
To think there was to him, of all his kind.
Alone such bliss assigned;
And presently began his thoughts to set
Awork how he should get
This thing he yearn'd for: for the man was poor
And hardly could procure
Fit sustenance. In study had he spent
His substance, being bent
On his strange hopes past thought of worldly gain.
But, as he rack'd his brain,
Awhile all fruitlessly, for means hereby
He should make shift to buy
The needed metal, that came nigh to be
The price of a squire's fee.

He suddenly bethought him that there yet,
Uncharged by any debt,
Remain'd to him one little piece of land,
Fruitful enough and spann'd
By the swift Loire; a little vine-set field
Whose fertile soil did yield
A dole of daily substance, scant enough
For all save those that plough
The fields of knowledge; earnt as the reward
Of his young blood outpour'd
On many a foughten field of sunny France;
Which, being sold, perchance
Might, with some curious arms he once had gain'd.
Whilom when Fortune deign'd
To favour him against his foe in fight.
Fulfil the sum aright
He needed to possess the thing he sought.
But if (O woeful thought!)
His substance being wasted in this wise.
His glorious enterprise
Should fail, for all his hopes and efforts? Why,
What could he do but die?
And to a fighter, death was terrorless.
While, if the Fates should bless
His long desire with the fulfill'd delight,
Would not his soul be quite
Absolved from life and its ignoble need.
Seeing that he should feed
On the fair food of an unearthly bliss
And with his love's best kiss
And in her sight from all the weary dearth
And stressfulness of earth
Be purified? So either hap might chance,
Ill or deliverance.
And in no wise should he have need again
Of that unlovely bane
Of our dull lives, that is our curse and stay.
Without which is no way
To live nor with it to live happily.
Wherefore his land sold he
And all his arms, except one suit of mail.
Wrought out with many a scale
And ring of steel, and his good sword and spear
And all the warlike gear
He had erst ridden to the battle in.
With age and use full thin
And rusty grown, but still of temper keen
And faithful, having been

A right good armourer's work of middle Spain;
And with the double gain
He bought a lump of virgin gold as large
As a Moor's battle-targe.
Wherewith to work the magic that he learnt
Within the scroll. There burnt
Within his breast so uncontroll'd a fire
And urgence of desire
To fill the measure of his high intent.
That scarce the day was spent,
Whereon he bought die gold, and in the sky
The moon was white and high.
Ere to the roof-top of his house he crept.
And there, whilst all folk slept.
In the full ripple of the flooding light.
Did work the livelong night.
To fashion out the ore with his own hands
Into smooth beaten bands
Of wroughten gold, moulding them circle-wise
Into such shape and guise
As for the seven days' journey should be meet
To guard his horse's feet
Against the highway's stones. The work did grow
Beneath his hands full slow
And tediously; for many a year was past
Since he had labour'd last
At such smith's craft; but yet the earnest will
Redeem'd the want of skill.
And with much toil at last the squire did make
The stubborn gold to take
Shoe-shape. All night he wrought beneath the moon.
And with the dawn the shoon
Fourfold were finish'd, round beyond impeach.
Pierced with four holes in each;
Nor, for the fitting, unto each did fail
The needful golden nail.
To clasp the circlet through the holes fourfold.
And so it chanced the gold
Was wholly spent, to the last glittering grain,
Nor did a speck remain
Of the thick ore, when the last nail was wrought;
Wherefore Squire Ebhart thought
The omen fair and braced his heart with it
Then, as the night did flit
Across the hilltops in the van of mom
And the pale lights were born.
That in the dawn do herald the young day.
Streaking the cheerless grey

Of heaven with their rose and opal woof,—
Descending from die roof,
Before the daybreak, hastily he dad
The harness, that he had
Yet left to him, upon his sturdy breast
And in his morion's crest
Set the strait plume he had been wont to wear
In the old days, once fair
And flaunting scarlet, but now faded sore.
Then did he strike the four
Worn shoes of iron from his horse's feet,
And in their stead the meet
Gold circlets set and beat them firmly on.
And now the steed must don
His harness and caparisons of war,
Such as of old he bore,
Chanfrein and poitrail with its rusty spike,
Rerebrace and all the like.
And so,—the twain addrest in everything
For knightly venturing
Needful and meet,—the man bestrode his horse;
And on the appointed course
The old squire sallied forth with his old steed.
As over hill and mead
The young day came with slow and timorous feet,
And the chill air grew sweet
With the clear dews and the pure early scent
Of the waked flow'rets, blent
For incense to the daybreak from the earth;
And in the tender birth
Of morning all things joy'd, and tunes were strong
Of larks' and linnets' song.
So, riding through the dim white streets, as yet
Unstirr'd by all the fret
And hum of daily labour, waking all
The echoes with the fall
Of his steed's hoofs upon the hilly way.
He came to where there lay
Before the gate the guardians of the town,
Upon the grass thrown down
To watch the portal, cross'd with many a bar
And bolt of steel. Ajar
The wide leaves stood, whilst sleep possessed the folk
So wholly, that the stroke
Of the squire's horse-hoofs stirr'd their slumbering
But as an echoing
Of sound in dreams, nor all his calling roused
Them anywise, so drowsed

With sleep they were.—And so he thought to make
His outward way, nor break
The warders' wide-mouth'd rest; but as he strove
The ancient gate to move
On its dull flanges, clogg'd with all the rust
Of many a year, and thrust
The half-dosed, ponderous leaves apart enough
To give him way, the gruff
Harsh creaking of the hinge that swung for him,—
Breaking upon the dim
Sleep-troubled senses of the folk that lay
Adream beside the way,—
With some faint mimic sound of buckler-dang
And foemen's trumpets, rang
Within the dull dazed channels of their brain.
Snapping the slumberous chain
Wherewith the dream-god held their heavy sense
In leaden-limb'd suspense;
So that they started up from sleep and saw
The squire, that in the raw
Chill morning dimness pass'd athwart the gate;
And wondering thereat,
Caught up bright arms and cried to him to stay.
But he, upon his way
Slackening not, faced round upon his seat,
That so their eyes might meet
A visage that they knew; and they, for friend
Recalling him, did wend
Back to their ward, with many a mutter'd oath,
Born of their thwarted sloth,
'Gainst him that so untimely broke their sleep.
But Ebhart down the steep
Of the fair hill rode, all unheeding them,
Whilst on the pearlèd hem
Of the fair sky the dim day brighten'd up
Into the azure cup
Of the sweet heaven, that lay on field and hill,
All rippleless, until
Its blue deeps broke upon the purple verge
Into a snowy surge
Of swan-breast cloudlets, laced with palest gold;
And then the shadows roll'd
Their mantles round them, and the lingering night
Fled from the coming light
And so uprose the golden-armour'd sun
And smote the ridges dun
Of the deep-bosom'd hills and kindled all
Their furrows tenebral

Into a wonderwork of luminous spires.
Hung with the fretted fires
Of dawning, and each crest in the pure light
Grew to a chrysolite
Of aspiration. On each upland lawn
Down fell the dewy dawn
And waked the flowers from their green-folded sleep,
And o'er each verdant steep
Of sloping greensward swept the sun-chased mist,
Ruby and amethyst
With pitiless sweet splendour. Every wood
With the sweet minstrel brood
Grew carolful, with, here and there, at first
A note, and then a burst
Of single song, soon swelling to a sea
Of choral ecstasy
And thanks for the young day and the delight
Of victory o'er the might
Of darkness; and each living thing that dwells
Within the cool wood-dells
Or in the meadows, to the awakening
Of that sweet day of Spring
Did homage. So rode Ebhart onward, through
The cool sweet tender blue
Of the fresh springtide dawning, glad at heart,
Following the rays that part
The morning sky to westward. By the edge,
Purple with flower'd sedge.
Of the dear stream, whose tinkling currents went
Toward the Occident,
The stout squire fared, through many a thymy field
With the fresh heaven ceil'd,—
Crush'd with his horsehoofs many a tender flower,
That in the sweet dawn hour
Open'd its gold and azure eyes from dreams
Of the near June's sunbeams.
And saw the kine regardant on the grass,
That aye, as he did pass
Across the greensward on his destrere true.
Wet to the hocks with dew,
Turn'd their slow heads to gaze upon the twain
Awhile, then back again
Bent down their muzzles with a lazy grace
To the rich pasture-place.
Thickset with flowers and juicy herbs. And then,—
About the hour when men
Are wont to go to labour and the light
Across the fields grows white

And large with full mid-morn,—the clear stream pass'd
The green sweet fields and fast
Among the emerald cloisters of a wood
Its farther course pursued.
Streaking the moss with brown and silver threads
And sprinkling the pale beds
Of primroses and windflowers, white and blue.
With its life-giving dew.
And in the ways the light grew dim again;
But through the leaves, like rain
Of gold, the sunshine broke and fell in showers
Upon the upturn'd flowers,
Whilst all the birds made curd to the May,
Answering the brooklet's lay
With choral thanks for all the cool sweet rills
It brought them from the hills.
And Ebhart, following the river's way.
Rode onward through the day
Along the fair green lapses of the wood.
With many a network strew'd
Of frolic sunbeams; and as he did £sire.
Full often was he ware
Of peeping hares and velvet-coated deer
That fled as he drew near,
And couchant fawns, upon the bracken set
For morning deep, as yet
Unknowing fright, that with great fearless eyes
Did gaze on him, childwise,
Questioning in themselves what this might be.
Clanking in panoply
Of rust-red mail along the ferny maze
Of the cool woodland ways.
The rabbits scamper'd from his horse's feet.
As o'er some wood-lawn, sweet
With hyacinths, he pass'd, or down some glen.
Purple with cyclamen;
And now and then, as through the wood he went.
On his strange hopes intent.
There met him some tann'd woodman, stout and bluff,
That with a word of gruff
Early day-greeting did accost the squire.
But else of his desire
No foreign harshness broke the pleasant spell.
Nor on his senses fell
A human sight or sound; but all was sweet
And silent, as is meet
For him that dreams in the fair midmost Spring,
Amid the birds that sing

And the fresh flowers that gladden the old world
With their pure eyes, impearl'd
In many a whorl of virginal faint green.
Slow wound the way between
The columns of the trees; and now and then
Some slope of shallowing glen
Ceased suddenly upon an open space.
Where many a fern did lace
The greensward and the heather put forth buds
And the red sad-eyed studs
Of pimpernels did diaper the grass.
Anon the squire did pass
Betwixt lush hedge-rows, riding on again
Along some country lane,
Tangled with briers and the early rose
And the white weed that blows
With fragrant flower-flakes in the flush of May, —

Whereon the shadows lay
Of the new-leafèd trees, that over it
A sun-fleck'd roof did knit
To ward it from the heat Now, as he went
Adown some steep descent
Or toil'd along some bridle-path, high hung
Betwixt thin woods that dung
Close to the brow of some tall diff-spur's steep.
His downward glance would sweep
Across gold plains and cities thick with men
And many a hollow glen.
Sweet with the blossom'd vines in many a row,
Toss'd seas of apple-snow
And dropping gold of fire-flowers. Then again,
As on the open plain
The pair paced on and felt the sun once more,
The fragrant breezes bore
To him the distant hum of men and life,
And the dear sounds were rife
In the far distance of the village bells;
And on the mossy fells,
In the blue sky-marge, lay within his sight
Some little town of white,
With roofs rose-gilded by the flooding sun;
For the noon had begun
To hover over hills and charm the air
Into the peace most fair
And stirless of the midday. On the wold
Slumber'd with wings of gold
The hours, and all things rested. Not a breath

Told of the late-left death
Of the sad winter; but the world was glad,
As if for aye it had
The fair possession of the lovely May.
And then again the way
Wound down into the wood, and from the dells
Gush'd up the perfumed swells
Of breath from violets bedded in the moss.
And many a hare would cross
The sunn'd green pathway with a sunbeam's speed;
And still the valiant steed
Paced on, unslackening. So went horse and man,
Until the sun began
To draw toward the setting and the West
Grew glorious on the crest
Of the dumb hills. And now the day did fold
Its mantle of deep gold
And purple for its death upon the hills.
And all the pomp, that fills
The tragedy of sunset with the glow
Of a king's death, did strow
The radiant heaven. So down sank the sun,
And so the day was done;
And in the Occident the silver horn
Of the pale moon was borne
Up in the gold-tinct watchet of the skies.
And one by one, the eyes
Of the unsleeping stars were visible
In the dear purple bell
Of that great blossom that we mortals name
God's heaven, and there came
The hush of sleep upon the lovely land.
The Dream-god went and fann'd
The air with flower-breathed breezes, and one knew.
In the clear sweep of dew.
The backward wind, that had been wandering o'er
The pleasant fresh-flower'd shore.
And now upon the breast of the dead day
Came back to die away
Into the stillness. Still the west was flush'd.
Until the day-birds, hush'd
By the prone night, gave place to those that hold
The even with the gold
Of their dear grieving song. The nightingale
Began to tell the tale
Of her great poet's sorrow, that is aye
New-born and may not die,
Being too lovely and too sad withal, —

For sorrow may not fall
Into the deeps of comfortable death.
As may the Summer's breath
And the fierce gladness of the July-tide,—
And to his plighted bride
The night-thrush piped, amid the plaited leaves.
And every thing that grieves
Melodiously for the dead day was fain
To fill the air again
With silver sadness. So the night fell down,
And in her mantle brown
All weary things addrest themselves to deep,
And over all, the deep
Sweet silence brooded Then the man was tired,
And eke his steed required
Some natural ministrance of rest and food.
So in the middle wood
The squire dismounted and with ears attent,
Sought for some stream that went
Between the trees; and speedily the plash
Of ripples, that did dash
And gurgle over pebbles, with a note
Of welcome nearness smote
Upon his hearing; and without delay
He came where o'er the grey
Of the moon-coloured mosses, trickled through
The grass-roots and the rue
A crystal rill, that to the wavering moon
Sang up its changeless tune
In the pale night. Thither the square did bring
His horse; then, by the sring
Kneeling, drank deep and long, and looking round.
Spied fallen on the ground
Great store of berries from a neighbouring tree.
So from the boughs did he
Gather the fruit, and finding it was meet
For human food, did eat
A handful of sweet berries, red and brown,—
And satisfied, lay down
By his tired horse, that had already laid
Himself beneath the shade
Of a great elm, upon the cushioned moss.
Crushing the flowers across
The twisted grass-stalks in the mossy sward,
For many a fragrant yard,
Beneath his weight; for all the earth was strewn
So thick, beneath the moon.
With all the Spring-tide heritage and dower

Of lovely weed and flower,
One might not tread there but the feet must crush
Many a sweet flower-flush
And broidery on the green earth's bridal gown.
So fell the midnight down;
And still Squire Ebhart, by his sleeping horse,
Mused of the next day's course,
And for the changeless thought of coming bliss.
Forgot to woo the kiss
Of the fair sleep that is all tired men's due.
But, at the last, the dew
Of slumber fell upon his heavy lids,
And the fair God, that bids
The dreamer to the far enchanted land,
Laid on his brows a hand
Of woven moonbeams; till the thoughts took flight
Into the brooding night,
And with a smiling face, the sleeper lay
And dreamt of many a day
Long lost behind the glimmering veils of time.
And in a golden dime
Went wandering through the dreamlands of his youth.
Under the sweet skies' ruth,
Link'd to his lady. So Squire Ebhart slept.
What time the slow night swept
Along the silver woodways and the hours
Folded their wings on flowers,
For peace of moonlight, till the moon 'gan fade
For break of day, that laid
Its cold grey hands upon the purple dusk
And from the hodden husk
Of the small hours drew forth the rosy bud
Of morning, all a-flood
With glittering dews: the golden dawn 'gan wake.
With many a rosy flake
And pearl of sungleams flung across the eaves;
And through the screen of leaves,
That overlay the place where Ebhart slept,
The frolic sunlight crept,
By help of some stray chinks within the woof
Of the green luminous roof,
And kissing all his face, as there supine
He lay, in frolic vine
And grass embow'red, warn'd him that day was come;
And then the awakening hum
Of the fresh wood and the bright tuneful dang
Of quiring birds, that sang
The reveillade of morning, with the gold

Of the broad sun-glow, told
His drowsy sense that it was morn again
And he too long had lain
In faineant slumber. Then did he arise
And from his heavy eyes
Brushing with drowsy hands the dust of sleep,
Awhile watch'd the light creep
Along the crests; then suddenly bethought
Him of the thing he sought
And how, if he would come to his desire.
Before the sun rose higher.
At once upon his forward way he must
Be fain. And so he thrust
His sleep from off" him and with gladsome heart
Addrest him to depart
Upon his second day of journeying.
So, stooping to the spring
That well'd up through the thyme-roots clear and cool,
He wash'd away the dull
Gross heaviness of night that lay on him
And standing on the brim
Of the brown rippled pool, he call'd his steed.
That in the neighbouring weed
Did graze; and at his call the faithful beast
Was fain to leave his feast
And to his side came splashing through the fount.
In haste. Then did he mount
Into the saddle without more delay,
And to find out the way
He should traverse, a second he did pause
Half doubtfully, because
The man with sleep was somewhat dazed nor knew
At first what path led due
Toward the setting and the golden west;
Then to the realms of rest.
That lie beyond the day, his face he set.
And spurr'd his horse. Not yet
The dew was sun-dried from the pearlèd grass,
As steed and man did pass
Along the windings of the forest ways.
Nor the faint scented haze.
That hovers in the vanward of the morn,
Over the flowers, had worn
Its shimmering webs away, for the sun-glare.
Into the thin blue air
That waves unseen between the noontide rays;—
For, seven long Spring days,
From earliest morning to the couchant sun,

Must Ebhart ride, nor shun
The long day's labour,—turning not aside
For aught that he espied
Of fair or tempting,—if he would possess
The yearn'd-for loveliness
Of his high dreams. So seven long days he rode
Along green pass and road.
From morning-glitter to the even-gloam.
Under the blue sky-dome.
Following his dream through many changing lands;
Now o'er the white sea-sands,
With horsehoofs splashing through the foamy spray
That broke across the way, —
Now passing through the till'd fair fields of men,
Hearkening to lark and wren
And all the fowls whose kindly use it is
Folk with the promised bliss
Of their sweet song, to hearten at their toil,—
Now riding where the soil
Blew thick and sweet with roses red and white.
And with the fair delight
Of minstrelsy the scented air was weft;
And whiles within the deft
Of many a bare rock and savage hill.
Whose rifts rich gems did fill
To overflowing and along whose veins
The red gold blazed, like stains
Of sunlight fix'd by some magician's skill.
Through many a mountain rill,
Swollen to torrents by the young year's rains,
And over blossom'd plains
Of heathy moorland, undefiled by feet
Of toiling men and sweet
With blowing breezes from the distant sea,—
Through deeps of greenery
And dim dumb churches of the giant pines.
Ranged in sad stately lines.
Waiting the coming of the Gods to be
To hail with hymns,—rode he
Unwearying alway; whilst the golden shoes
Each day some part did lose
Of their soft metal on the pointed stones;
For all along the cones
Of many a mountain range he toil'd, whereo'er
No foot had pass'd before.
Save that of goat or deer,—through many a reach
Of grey and shingly beach
And many a flinty pass; nor might aside

Turn from the highway's wide
Rough band of white, that wound out far away
Into the dying day.
To seek the tender greensward of the meads
That lay beside him. Needs
Must he endure the utmost of the toil,
The bitterest of the coil
Of struggles and of hardships, that abode
Upon' his wishward road.

II.

ATTAINMENT

And now six days of journeying were done,
And eke the seventh one
Drew tow'rd the hour when, in the middle day,
The golden lights do stay
Their upward travel in the slant blue sky,
And all the plains do lie
Asleep beneath the sun. And with the flame
Of noon, a change there came
Upon the forward path; for until then
The squire's advance had lain
Through plains and woods and countries known to man
But now the road began.
Upon the nooning of the seventh day,
To merge into a way
Strange beyond any that a man could know.
Upon the earth below
Strange glittering shells and sands of gray were strown.
And many a blood-red stone,
Changeful in colour; and above, gnarl'd trees
Shook with an unfelt breeze;
And therein many a shape of dwarf and gnome.
Such as, folk say, do roam
About the dreamland's gates, did climb and ding,
Mowing and gibbering
Like uncouth monstrous apes. On either hand,
Gray flowerless plants did stand
Along the highway's marge, and blood-red bells.
Such as for midnight spells
Thessalian witches pluck: and thereabout
Crowded a noiseless rout
Of gray and shadowy creatures. All the air
Was misted with the glare
Of the curst flowers and the strange baleful scent

That from the herbs was sprent
As for some ill enchantment: and the things
That hover'd there had wings
And waver'd dimly over Ebhart's head
And beckon'd as they sped
Across his path, striving to draw him off
From the highway most rough
And rude, among the pleasant fields that lay
Each side the rugged way,—
Tempting the man with many-colour'd flowers
And semblants of lush bowers
Of trellised foliage, set beside the path
In many a waving swath
Of com and greensward, easeful to behold,—
Wooing him in the gold
Of the rich meadows to lie down and sleep
Away, in that green deep
Of flowers, the weariness of his long ride.
But Ebhart not aside
A hair's-breadth turn'd his steed for all their wiles,
Nor for the golden smiles
Of the fair harbours that invited him.
Swerved from the highway's rim,
Clear cut against the far horizon's blaze
Of gold, his steadfast gaze;
But with a firm-set mouth rode on thereby.
Watching the sun now nigh
To death upon the hills, as one that sees
In thought his miseries
Draw to their term, and for no thing nor power
Will, in that fateful hour,
Draw bridle nor be tempted from his road«
So ever he abode
In the due westward path, regarding not
The glamours any jot,
That compass'd him about. Then those strange things,
That with their blandishings
And spellwork strove to tempt him to forego
His long intent, did know
Their efforts void and with a doleful cry
Evanish'd utterly
Into the twilight and were no more seen.
And as they fled, the treen
Grew green again; the grey herbs withered off
And all the sky did doff
The lurid gloom and hazes that it wore.
But Ebhardt, conning o'er
The dim-gold landscape and the purple west

For tokens of his quest.
E'en as he rode, o'er in his memory turn'd
The things for which he yearn'd, —
That of the dreams which had possest his youth
There might no whit, in sooth.
Be lost for lack of his remembering:
And so, as with swift wing
His spirit wander'd in the olden ways,
Searching amid the maze
Of memories thick-woven in his mind,—
The hurrying thoughts were twined
Into the fulness of the old desire;
And with the ancient fire
There grew within the chambers of his brain,
Unchanged by years and pain.
The flower-new fantasies of days gone by.
Now was the time to die
Come for the day, wearied to utterest
Of life, Hyenas the west
Kiss'd its last kiss against the pale sun's lips;
And now, as the eclipse
Of the red light left void the weeping blue
Of the pale heaven and through
The woven cloisters of the purpled trees
The evening-waken'd breeze
Began to flutter,—upon either hand
Over the weary land,
Faint music sounded from the dim sweet woods,
And the delight that broods
Over fill'd sleep was sweet upon the squire:
And all the man's desire
As 'twere to brim with ecstasy, he heard
The carol of a bird,
That sang as it awhile had dwelt among
The high seraphic throng
And listened to the smitten golden lyres
Pulsing among the choirs
Of Paradise, beside the crystal sea,—
And such an ecstasy
Of echoes lingered at its heartstrings still.
It never could fulfil
Its bliss with memory of those wondrous hours.
But to the earthly flowers
Some snatches of the singing's rise and fall
Strove ever to recall
Then in the middle road there rose before
The squire a mist, that wore
Strange blazonry of many mingling hues,

As 'twere the falling dews
Were curtain'd in a thick and glittering haze
Across the forward ways;
And in the clear sweet hour before the night
There rose in the twilight
An arch of glitterance upon the hem
Of heaven, like a gem
Built to a rainbow, that 'twixt earth and sky
Grew higher and more high;
And as it grew, the colours that it wore
Shone glorious ever more,
As if it were the portal of the land
Of Faerie. Nigh at hand
The place beyond that archway oi a dream
Unto the squire did seem.
And with great joyance through the bended bow,
That all the earth did strow
With blending lights of amethyst and gold,
He rode, thinking to hold
His dream at once; but, as he pass'd the verge,
The mountains seem'd to surge
In the blue distance like a billowy sea,
And the far sky did flee
Along the arch. The golden heaven's rim
Grew paler and more dim.
Receding alway, and the place whereon
He rode was clad upon
With a bright sudden growth of magic blooms.
Out of the folding glooms
Of the near dusk rose trail on trail of flowers
And arch'd the road with bowers
Of an unearthly sweetness, marking out
His way, beyond a doubt.
Unto his quest: and as he rode along
The vaulted path, the song
Of the strange bird more rapturous ever grew,
Like an enchanted dew
Of music falling in a silver sea.
All over flower and lea
A new light pass'd, that was not of the sun.
For all the day was done
And the dim night held all the lands aswoon.
Until the hornèd moon
Should ride pearl-shod across the purple wold.
Then from the rim of gold
That lingered still on the horizon's marge,
A golden Maze grew large
Of glamorous colour and within the span

Of the broad arch began
To spread and hold the purple of the skies;
And as with all his eyes
Gazed Ebhart, wonder-dumb,—against the ground
Of purest gold that crown'd
The heavens in the ending of the glade.
There were for him inlaid
Turrets and battlements, a flowering
Of every lovely thing.
Along the marge of the sweet sky there rose
Gold towers and porticoes
Of burnish'd jasper, ruby cupolas
And domes high-hung, topaz
And opal-vaulted; sapphire campanelles
Held up their flower-blue bells
Against the gold sky; silver fountain-jets
Between the minarets
Threw high their diamond spray, and fretted spires
Flamed up, like frozen fires
Of amethyst and beryl, past the height
Of lofty walls of white.
Thickset with terraces aflame with flower.
Shower upon scented shower.
The blossoms rain'd from high and bloomy trees,
Before a scented breeze.
That fill'd the air with balms and orient gold
And on its waftings roll'd
Across the plains a singing sound of lyres.
Smitten from golden wires.
And clarion-notes, wide-spreading like a sea
Under a company
Of joinèd voices, murmuring softest words
To music like white birds
Winnowing the foam of some gold Indian bay.
Lay murmur'd unto lay
From out that dwelling of a God's delight,
Following each other's flight
To greet the dreamer with their blissful stress,
And pipes and lutes no less
Yearn'd up to him with strains of welcoming.
And Ebhart, lingering
As 'twere before his nigh-fulfill'd desire,
Knew all those towers of fire,
Sun-glancing, and the flower-fleck'd terraces,
And in the harmonies,
Wide-winging through the crystal air agleam
With gold-flakes, knew his dream.
As of old times he had pourtray'd the place.

With all its changeful grace
No moment same, for all the golden dew
And all the flowers that blew
And shimmer'd like a noon-mist thereabout.
So with a glad heart, out
Through the flower-arch he rode and came unto
The portal, sculptured through
With pictures of a dream in chrysoprase
And beryl and a maze
Of blossoms of the jewel that in one
Is flower and precious stone,
Being clear hyacinth,—wroughten by no hand
Of man. The leaves did stand
Wide-open for his coming, backward roll'd
Even to their flange of gold.
So in he rode and saw the white town spread.
In all its goodlihead
Like nothing earthly, very still and wide.
Upon his either side
Far-stretching like a vision of the night
Beyond his further sight.
The place was overrun with flowerage
Of wondrous Nooms that wage
War with the sun in many an Orient clime:
Great silver bells did climb
The gabled turrets with their linking chains,
Mix'd thick with crimson skeins
And chalices of sapphire. In the ways
Gold-paven, rose a maze
Of trellised porticoes and white dream-steads;
And midst the mossy beds
Of the lush flowers, strewn like a rain of stars
In every court, through bars
Of gold one saw clear lakelets lay and toy'd
With the white swans, that joy'd
To sport in their cool pleasance; and the air
Was tuneful with the fair
Clear tinkle of the crystal rills that ran
Across each flowerbed's span
And fed the grass-roots. Then, as down the street
Rang out the horse's feet,
Calling strange lovely echoes from their cells,
Flute-notes and silver bells.
That broke the silence with a songful spray,
There ran in the mid way
Unto the man a sudden cloud of girls.
With breasts like double pearls
Rose-tinted by long sojourn in the gold

Of some far Orient, stoled
But in the waving mantles of their hair:
Tall maidens, dusk and fair
With the long gilding kisses of the light,
Fresh from the fierce delight
Of plains of golden Ind and Javan seas.
Shook on the fragrant breeze
Rich scents from lotus-cups; and Grecian maids,
Under their night-black braids,
Cinct with the green acanthus, did advance,
link'd in a rhythmic dance:
Fair girls came, crown'd with white narcissus-stars,
From rose-strewn plains of Fars;
The lithe mild maids of gold Pacific isles
Brought him their pearly smiles
And olive brows set clear with eyes of black:
Nor to his sight did lack
Women with faces of the rosy snow
Only the west can show.
In whose fair ivory for double light
Two tender eyes and bright
Were set, the colour of the spring-sky's blue,
Hazed with the early dew,—
And down their shoulders fell a fleece of gold.
In many a ripple roll'd
Of sun-imprisoning locks. And these beside,
From every portal's wide
Gaped folds came out into the golden street.
Eager the man to greet.
Bright shapes of every radiant eye-delight
Of lovely women dight
In pleasant raiment, that a dream can heap
Up in the aisles of sleep.
Then those fair creatures,—waving like a sea
Of gold and ebony.
For all the mazes of their floating hair,—
Smote the clear jewell'd air
With songs of triumph and of welcoming;
And while their lips did sing,
Their hands strew'd jasmines in the horse's path
And with a scented swath
Of violet and rose and orange-stars.
Hid every sign of wars
And toil that cumberèd the valiant steed.
Now in the song indeed
And in the varied beauty of the girls,
Set dear in clustering curls,
Were easance and delight for any man

That since the world began
Loved girls 'and song and the soft cadenced beat
Of golden-sandall'd feet
On thick-strewn flowers; and there might well the fire
Of any man's desire
Be quell'd and satisfied with loveliness
And all its dreams possess
In those fair women, with their flowery kiss
And their descant's clear bliss.
But Ebhart cherish'd in his heart—made clear
By many a weary year
Of void desire—the memory of a face
Of an unearthly grace
And glory, that had smiled on him in dreams.
Woven, it seem'd, of gleams
Of pure spring suns and flowers of white moonlight,—
And for the memory, might
Have pleasance in no woman save in this.
That was his Beatrice
And queen of love. So all unmoved he went
By any blandishment
Of that fair throng, slowly adown the street,
Hoping his eyes should meet
Her eyes for whom alone his heartstrings shook.
Then, seeing that the look
Of yearning died not from the seeker's eyes.
Circling in bright bird-wise.
The fair crowd broke before his onward route;
And from the rest came out
A maiden, robed in falling folds of green
And crown'd with jessamine
And myrtle-snows, that took his bridle-rein
And led the steed, full fain.
Along the fragrant carpet of the way.
Toward a light that lay
Far in the westward distance like a flame.
Of gold. Behind them came
The frolic crowd of girls, following the twain
With showers of blossom-rain
And rills of song, until they brought them where
Pillars of pearl upbare
A dome of lustrous sapphire, flank'd with spires
That pierced the sky like fires
Up-flaming from the molten furnaces
Of middle earth, 'mid trees
Ablaze with flowers of gold. Before the gate
The maiden did abate
Her onward way and bade the squire alight

Then on the pavement, white
With scented snows, the man sprang lightly down
And with his gauntlet brown
Smote on the golden trellis such a stroke,
That all the echoes woke
Thereto: and therewithal the gold leaves split
In twain and did admit
The sight through archways into many a glade
Of gardens, all outlaid
Beneath the heavens' kisses. Entering
Therein, the maid did bring
The squire, through many dwellings of delight.
Into a place where light
Lay full and soft a velvet sward athwart.
There in the middle court
Circled with jewell'd cloisters all around,—
Upon the emerald ground
Of guilded mosses broider'd with all flowers
In stories of the hours
That through the spring and summer bear the year
Over the flower-beds clear,—
There was a throne of gold and coral set,
With many a goodly fret
Of ivory work, upon the suppliant heads
Of strange fair quadrupeds.
Most like a lovely lion with girl's eyes.
Upborne; and warder-wise
About the throne, stood maidens white as milk,
Vestured in snowy silk
Banded with cramozin, and pages fair,
Clad all in pleasant vair
And silver, that so thick and numberless
About the throne did press.
One might not see the visage of die Crown'd
That sat thereon. Around,
Among the roses and the tulip-beds,
Thick-vein'd with silver threads
Of tiny trickling rills, fair birds of white
And red did stalk and bright
Peacocks and doves of every lovely hue,
Golden and green and blue,
Trail'd jewell'd plumes along the garden-ways,
That with the goodly blase
Of their full splendour so did fill the bower,
It seem'd all fairest flowers
Had put on wing and motion, to fulfil
Their beauty at the will
Of some enchantress of the olden days.

About the glancing ways
Of that bright garden ceaselessly they went,
Weaving its ravishment
Into fresh webs of colour and delight
And as their pageant bright
Eddied and wound among the garden-grots.
From all their fluted throats
There was a vaporous choral song exhaled.
As 'twere the spirit fail'd
Within them, for delight, to shape its bliss
Into the words that kiss
The ear with perfect music, and was fain
For very rapturous pain
Of ecstasy to lapse into a song.
Now on the glittering throng
Long time the squire had gazed, held in a trance
Of joy, nor dared advance
His spell-bound feet; and oft for bliss he sigh'd.
But that fair maid, his guide,
Laid hands on him and brought him, through the crowd
Of maidens snowy-brow'd.
To the mid-garden, where the throne was set
Then did the man forget
All things that blazon'd earthly life for him.
And all his dream grew dim
Before a new-born wonder: for, as there
He stood, he was aware
Of a fair shape that sat upon the throne,
Such as to him was shown
In dreams the image of his Queen of Love.
Clear was her brow above
The crystals of the snow for purity.
And round its ivory
Seven silver stars there were for diadem
Upon the waving hem
Of the rich tresses set, that rippled down,
A flood of golden-brown,
The colour of the early chestnut's robe.
When yet the summer's globe
Is but half rounded out with flower and sun.
And from the stars did run
Commingling rays of many-colour'd light.
That with a strange delight
Fill'd all the trancèd network of her hair,
Wherein for all men's care
Were set soft anodynes and balms of sleep.
Within her lips, a deep
Of coral garner'd up its pearls a-row,

And in her arching brow
There were two eyes unfathomable set,
Wherein might one forget
The glance of the dead friend of bygone years
And the sweet smile through tears
Of the lost love of youth; for they were clear
And soft as a hill-mere
After spring-rains, whenas the early dew
Has fallen in its blue,
And yet with some strange hints of deeper tones,
Such as the June night owns.
Before the moon is full, when the clear stars
Ride on their jewell'd cars,
Queenless, across the purple of the skies
And the day-murmur dies
Under the vaulted dome of amethyst
With such lips Dian kiss'd
Endymion sleeping on the Latmian sward:
From such twin eyes were pour'd
The philtres of the summer night upon
The evil-fortuned son
Of Priam, smitten with a fearful bliss.
Whoever had the kiss
Of her red lips kiss'd never woman more.
Having attained the shore
Of that supernal bliss the ancients sought
So long, but never wrought
To find,—the very perfectness of love.
Upon one hand, a dove.
Pearl-white and with a golden colleret,
Was for a symbol set,
And in the other one lys-blooms she held.
Gold-cored and snowy-bell'd,
The sceptre of her queendom. Twixt the snows
Of her fair breast, a rose,
Mix'd red and white, lay droop'd with heavy head.
As with the mightihead
Of love that fill'd her presence all forspent
And as on him was bent
That foil sweet visage, its sheer perfectness
Of glory did possess
The squire with such a wondering delight
Of bliss and such a might
Of hurrying thoughts, that for the very fire
Of his fulfill'd desire
The life well-nigh forsook him; and eftsoon
He would have fallen aswoon
Before that Lady of all loveliness,

That from the ardent stress
And furnace of his dream to shape had grown.
But she, to whom were known
The passions that within his soul did meet,
Descending from her seat.
Bent down and in her ivory arms embraced
His neck and all enlaced
His failing visage with her woven hair.
Holding him captive there
Within a gold and silver prison house.
Then, parting from the brows
His ruffled hair, she kiss'd him on the mouth;
And suddenly the drouth
Of yearning, that so many years had tried
His spirit, did subside
And was all quench'd within a honied deep
Of kisses, that did steep
His soul in ravishment ineffable
And restful. So there fell
A woof of sleep upon his every limb;
And in the trances dim
Of twining dreams, he heard a silver song
From out that glittering throng
Of lovely girls and jewel-plumaged birds
Fill all the air with words.
That (if with devious weary earthly speech
One might avail to reach
Some echo of their sweetness) in this wise
Somewhat did fall and rise,
Like sea-waves beating on a golden bar
Of sands, but lovelier far.

Song

Low laid in thyme
And nodding asphodels,
Dream on and feel fiower-fragrance kiss
Thy forehead free from all the dints of time:
Thou shall awake to greater bliss,
Bounden with linkèd spells
Of love and rhyme.

Fear not, pale friend,
Thy dream shall pass away:
Thou hast attained the shores of rest,
Where the wave-break against the grey beach-bend
Brings up sad singings from the West

No more. Here Love is aye
Sweet without end.

For here the grief
And sadness left behind
With weary life are turned to gold
Of dreams: from stern old mem'ries, sheaf on sheaf,
The buds of strange delights unfold
Their sweets, like flowers we find
Under a leaf.

Here in this deep
Of grass-swaths, piled with flowers,
All things most fair and loveliest,
Too pure for earth and all her toil to reap,
Do lie and crush the fruits of rest,
And all the golden hours
Lie down to sleep.

Here Lave doth sit,
No longer sad and cold,
As in the weary life of men
The hard stern need of toil has fashioned it;
But pure and silver-clear again
And withal red as gold
For crownals fit.

Here hope is not,
Nor fear: for all the ease
One wearied for in wordly strife
Were but as nought beside one pearly grot
Of this fair place, and all a life
Of fears herein would cease
And be forgot.

Hath any dole?
Bird-songs are comforting,
And all the flower-scents breathe of balm:
Dream on and soothe the sadness from thy soul;
For here life glitters like a calm
Of summer seas that sing
A barcarolle.

Count life with flowers!
This is our dial here.
A kiss and violets twined around
The browy soft sleep in honeysuckle bowers,
Lilies and love with roses crown'd,

Jasmine and eglatere,
Cadence our hours.

Dream within dream;
Dreaming asleep, awake;
There is no sweeter thing than this,
To lie beneath flower-snows and fountain-gleam,
Save if with touch of lips and kiss
One win the sleep to break,
Yet hold the dream.

III.

FALLING AWAY

So the song hover'd over Ebhart's sleep,
By many a silver sweep
And many a golden sigh of horns and flutes
And broidery of lutes
Within the failing cadences sustained:
Andy as he slept, the stain'd
Worn harness and accoutrements from him
Were borne, and every limb
Was purified from all the dust of toil
And all that journey's soil.
In essences of all the balms that be
In Ind or Araby
For purging all life's weary stains and sad.
Then on the man was clad
Fair raiment, thrice in Tyrian purples dyed,
Gold-fringed and beautified
With broidery of pearl-work silver-laced;
And on his breast they placed
A golden owch, rare-wrought and coral-chain'd.
And as the singing waned,
The magic slumber slid away from him;
And therewithal the dim
Sad doubts and weariness of earth forwent
His soul and there was lent
To every limb a perfectness of ease.
As in the golden seas
Of some charmed ocean he had bathed and cast
His age off. So he past
With that fair queen athwart the dreamy land.
Wandering, hand in hand,
Through many courts and jewel-vaulted halls.
Wherein the trellis'd walls

Show'd through the sunflecks,—carved and limnèd o'er
With all the lovely lore
Of Faerie and all the glitterance
Of Orient romance;
And in one chamber,—thick with jasmine stars
Woven betwixt the bars
Of gold that latticed all the sides from floor
To roof-tree, vaulted o'er
With one clear bell of sapphire silver-ray'd,—
Them side by side they laid
On beds of sandal wood and cramozin;
Then did fair maids bring in
A banquet, set and sweet in golden shells,
Mingled with great flower-bells
And cups of jasper and corneliand.
There peacocks did expand
Their jewell'd fans, fresh from the fairy looms;
Herons with argent plumes,
Untorn by falcon, lay on silver beds;
And opal-blazon'd heads
Of dove and culver glitter'd out through green
Of bedding moss. Between
Gold lilies lay the silver-feather'd swan,
Reclined in death upon
Lush leaves of vine and flowers of oranges;
And every bird that is
For pleasant food ordain'd, in vine leaves wet
With crystal dew, was set
Before the twain, each in its several room.
And from the jewell'd gloom
Of ocean-deeps there came its lovely things.
Gold fish with silver wings.
Great diamond-sided carp with opal eyes.
Dolphin that ever dies
A rainbow glory and an eye-delight;
Sword-fish, and shell-fish bright
With ruby armour, mullets gold and grey.
And all the rest that play
Among the hyacinthine cool sea-deeps—
Where many a coral creeps
'Mid pearls and weeds of every lovely hue—
Until themselves endue
The radiance of the pearl and coral things
And the dear colourings
Of feather'd sea-flowers thick about their life:
These all and more were rife.
Outlaid—for food of men to godship grown—
In many a precious stone

Wroughten with silver to the mimic cup
Of that fair flower that up
From the still lake holdeth its argent star.
That men call nenuphar.
There did the beehives yield their amber dew.
Glittering pale golden through
The frail white fretwork of the honeycomb;
And in their velvet bloom
Shone gold and purple fruits of the year's prime.
That in the Autumn-time
Of some far wondrous land had hung and glow'd,
What while the winter rode
On his pale horse across the stricken earth;
And the clear soul of mirth
And love was there in chalices of wine,
Such as no earthly vine
Has ever dreamt of in its dreams of June;
And all the place was strewn
With jewels full of juices wonder-sweet,
That seem'd for kings more meet
To wear upon their brows, than to suffice.
Even in Paradise,
Unto men's hunger. Over all there fell
A shower of asphodel
And almond-blossoms, and the air did rain
With roses. So the twain
Lay at the banquet upon lavish flowers,
Whilst through the gradual hours
Bright sights and sounds did charm the time's advance
For them. One while, a dance
Of wood-nymphs glitter'd circlewise across
The windflower-sprinkled moss,
That paved the halls; or from the fountain's deep
Of silver sands would sweep
A flight of green-hair'd naiads, dripping gold
And pearls from every fold
Of their wet hair and weed-ytangled dress;
And then, perchance, the stress
Of silver clarions and the sweet sad thrill
Of the struck harps would fill
The air, preluding to a cavalcade
Of lovely shapes array'd
In cramozin and azure,—dames and knights
And all the eye-delights
Of the old pageantries of queens and kings;
And to the cadenced strings
And reeds swell'd up the dash of shields and spears
And the fair tranceful fears

Of the bright battle and the hot tourney:
The clang of the sword-play
Rang out from targe and morion, and the ring
Of lance-points shivering.
The banners and the tabards ebb'd and flow'd.
The jewell'd crownals glow'd
In tireless changeful splendour; and the haze
Of the far-column'd ways
Glittered with glancing mail and blazonries
Of all bright hues one sees
In the fair pictures of the olden time.
And oft with many a rhyme
The minstrels fill'd the pauses, in quaint lays
And songs of bygone days
Hymning the praise of many a champion
Of time past So slid on
The dream along the halls of phantasy,
Folding him blissfully
Within a rapturous calm; but, more than this,
That crownèd lady's kiss,
The woven magic of her tresses' gleam
And her soft eye's sunbeam,
Fetter'd the dreamer in a silken trance
Of masterful romance.
Now, as the meal was done with many a song
And luting from the throng
Of pearl-limb'd girls,—the curtains of the dark
About the golden ark
Of the day-heaven were drawn; and the clear night
Came with its own delight
Of lambent stars and heavy night-flowers' scent,—
Whenas the firmament
Hangs o'er the earth like some great orange-grove
Wherethrough the fire-flies rove
In some far land of Orient,—to enspell
The senses; and the bell
Of the slant sky grew hung with fretted lights.
For never fail the night's
Enchantments in the land of dreams (as say
Some makers) nor the day
With its sheer splendours satisfies the sense;
But the easeful suspense
Of the stilled midnight is as welcome there
As morning, being fair
And full of lovely spells of peace and rest.
Graven on the palimpsest
Of day with star-runes; nor without the night
Could one have love's delight

In perfect fulness. So the night was spread
Above the golden bed
Of those two lovers, whilst the barefoot hours
Fled through the rosy bowers
Of that fair dream-stead, on the moonlight's wings;
And all the lovely things,
That fill the interspace betwixt sundown
And the new-risen crown
Of morning throned upon the Orient crests,
Hover'd about the breasts
Of that fair lady, as she lay asleep,
Folded in peace as deep
As the blue heaven with the gold stars fleck'd.
And when the morning check'd
His coursers for the sweep into the sky
And from the bravery
Of newborn day the glamours of the night
Folded their wings for flight
Where through the dusk the sun had made a gap,
Those lovers from the lap
Of their sweet slumbers rose and hand in hand,
Look'd over the fair land
And saw the eternal spring grow young again
Over each hill and plain
Of that enchanted paradise of sweets:
And the delight, that beats
To amorous tunes within the spring-flower blood,
Swelled up to overflood
Their quick'ning spirits with a radiant mist
Of philtres; and they kiss'd
Again with double rapture. In mid-green,
Under tall stately treen,
In noble woods they wander'd, where the birds
Hail'd them with golden words,
Clearer and lovelier than earthly song;
And all the pure-eyed throng
Of wood-flowers held sweet converse for their ease.
The blue anemones
Murmur'd quaint tender fairy-tales of spring
And of the blossoming
Of elfin souls in every pale sweet bod;
The fragile bells that stud
The moss with cups of sapphire, when the year
Brings round the Midsummer,
Sang mystic songs for them of summer nights
And all their deep delights
Of throbbing stars and singing nightingales;
And heather-bells told tales

Of elfins dancing on the thymy sward.
What while the white moon pour'd
Full hands of pearl upon the breezy moors.
And as along the floors
Of spangled moss they went, beneath the woofs
Of leaves, the tiny hoofs
Of deer smote softly on the woodland lawns.
And the lithe brown-eyed fawns
Laid velvet muzzles on their toying hands.
Now along golden sands
By sapphire deeps they walk'd, thick strewn with shells
Of each bright kind that dwells
In seas, and watch'd the gold fish dart and flash
Across the cool wave-plash
And the curl'd foam slide up and fall away
Into a silver spray.
As the great plangent waves broke, green and white.
In sheets of malachite.
Then would the queen take Ebhart by the hand
And from some jut of sand
Down diving through the gold and emerald waves.
Visit the coral caves
Of the sea-nymphs and all the palaces
Of crystal, under seas
Built for the Nereids' pleasance,—wandering
Along the deeps that ring
With mermaids' song, and plucking living flowers
That in the mid-sea bowers
Wave for the mermen, gold and blue and white.
Or with a calm delight
The twain lay floating on the silver foam,
Watching the azure dome
Of heaven wide-ceil'd above the emerald leas,
And the light fragrant breeze
Wafting the silver cloud-plumes o'er the blue.
Haply, some bird that flew,
Wide-winging, tow'rd the golden-stranded East,
Sometime its travel ceased
At her command, and in her ivory breast
Nestling, awhile would rest
And murmur stories of the wondrous things
Each day of wing-work brings
To one that pulses toward the rising sun.
And when the morn was done,
Mayhap, returning to the land, the queen
Within some heart of green
Would sit and hold the man within her arms.
Weaving with many charms.

For him to living shape and lovely sooth.
The memories of youth
And the quaint fancies of his wildest dreams.
Re-clad with golden beams
Of mystic splendour, ever fresh and new;
So that but now he knew
How very full his every thought had been
Of all the lovely sheen
And glamour of the land of phantasy.
Over the dappled lea
And the slant hillside, blossom-starr'd, would rise
Before his ravish'd eyes
Fair crystal castles and enchanted bowers,
Trellised with magic flowers,
That in their every calyx held a face
Of an unearthly grace.
Horn-notes came faint and far upon the breeze;
Between the moss-clad trees
Fair ladies pass'd, with greyhounds falcon-eyed
And pages at their side;
And knights rode forth a-questing. O'er the sward
Pageant on pageant poor'd
Of the quaint elves that hold the ancient woods
And the gnarl'd race that broods
Deep in the jewell'd chambers of the rock:
Or with her milk-white flock
Some dreamy shepherdess went sauntering by.
With flowerful hands and eye
Fix'd on the petals of some rose of gold.
And now the lilies told
The twain that day drew fast toward the dark.
Then did they both embark
In some fair shallop's pearl and ivory side.
And down the glancing tide
Of some full river, over-hung with trees.
Glided before the breeze
That fill'd the silken sails; 'twixt terraced walls,
Past rows of ancient halls
And towers far-glancing 'gainst the golden sky;
Where all the courts did lie
Ungated, and the dying sun sloped slow
Along the evening glow
Through range on range of golden palaces.
Glittering on lattices
Of blue and silver, tenantless and still.
A strange sad peace did fill
The lonely streets; and through the voiceless air,
Perchance, some breeze would bear

The silver sound of bells, whose music spread
In circles overhead,
Widening far out upon a stirless sea
Of silentness. Maybe,
Bytimes, the man would deem himself alone
In some fair meadow, strown
With bright-eyed flowers, or on some river's bank.
Where rank on plumèd rank
Sedges blew purple; when, as he did deem,
That sovereign of his dream
Had for a little faded from his side:
And at the first he sigh'd
To find her place left empty suddenly;
But soon he knew that she
Was ever with him, if invisible.
Whether some cowslip's bell
He idly broke or pull'd a violet up.
Straightway from out the cup
A sweet face look'd; two tender dewy eyes
Gazed deep in his, and sighs
Of ravishing sweet music fill'd his ears.
Until his soul with tears
Of joy brimm'd over: then two lips would seek
His own, as 'twere to speak
All things' love to him in a fragrant kiss;
And ravish'd with the bliss,
He would press closelier on the flower and find
It was his lady twined
Soft arms about him and laid lips to his
With such a flower-bell kiss.
Being both flower and bird and breeze and queen.
Or,—look'd he in the green
Of some fair crystal pool all fringed with sheaves
Of the nesh flower that weaves
Soft green and rosy-white of blooms around
Each lake that in the swound
Of the mid-June lies stirless,—there would grow
From out the deeps a snow
Of starry lily-petals, that, between
Their golden-gaufred green
Unfolding, show'd to him a tender face,
Crown'd with a dripping grace
Of gold-brown hair, that through the waves rose high.
Upon his lips to sigh
The soul of amorous longing. Being seen
Full, it was still the queen,
That in no wise could let man's love grow cold.
Being so manifold

And rich of heart, that as each flower she knew
To love, or as the dew
Wooeth the moonbeam's kisses: she could take
All shapes of love that wake
Under the skies: whether the nightingale
Telleth her amorous tale
Unto the argent-blossom'd thorn, the winds
About the pale woodbinds
Flutter with loveful longing, or the bees
Around the anemoaes
Fly with a bridal murmur; she could win
Her eyes to looks akin
And prison all their passion in her lays;
And in all other ways
Wherein on earth is love made manifest—
So that each loveliest
And peerless for the hour of love should seem—
That lady of a dream
Could twine the souls of mortals with delight
Nor with the deathless light
Of love alone was Ebhart's being blest:
Around his footsteps pressed
An ever-changing sea of lovely things;
The radiant flowerings
Of all the poet-hopes a dreamer knows.
While yet the dewy rose
Of his fresh youth is wormless for the years;
The wraiths of the waste tears
And the pure phantoms of the dear dead past
Came back to him at last
In a new guise of shapes emparadised:
For nothing it sufficed
Unto the perfecting of his desire
Of old, that for the squire
The happy shapes alone of his strange dreams—
Woven all of sunbeams
And griefless flowers—should be fulfilled for him:
He must possess the dim
Ethereal sadnesses that were so sweet,
Before the stem years' feet
Crush'd all the glory from the soul of pain;
And in his sight again
Must the impalpable essence new abide.
Sublimed and glorified
By the transfiguring splendour of his dream:
The much-loved dead must seem
To walk with him the blossom-trellis'd ways,
And the remember'd gaze

Of the dead friends he loved in days gone by
Meet him in every eye
Of flower-cups blinking on the mossy leas;
And in each fragrant breeze
Belovèd voices murmur him again
Old songs of love and pain
And hope undying. So the man did move
In one long dream of love,
And all his life was one great fairy-tale,
Wherein no thing did fail
Of the bright visions he had wont to see
In his fresh youth.—Ah me!
That joy should be so strong and pitiless
And mortal men no less
Inapt to brook its agony of sweets!
That the delight which beats
In the full veins should be the enemy
Of this frail flesh! That we
Should ever prove so uncreate to bear
The things that are most fair
In our idea,—should faint and die before
The dream of bliss is o'er!
Alas! we can bear sorrow and the stress
Of earth's dull weariness,
Day after day eating our bitter bread,
Silent, with tears unshed
And life still pulsing dumbly; but the kiss
Of the full rapturous bliss
We dream of withers us with its delight;
And back into the night
Of our despair needs must we faint and fall,
Finding dull custom's thrall
And the dumb pain of daily life less keen
And deadly than the sheen
Of the bright bliss to us unbearable!
So it to Ebhart fell
That he must be divorced from the delight
That with such godlike might
Of will he had prevail'd to win,—being strong
To dare and to prolong
His day in strife, cheer'd by some distant hope
Dim-radiant in the scope
Of the dull daily sky,—but not enough
Strong for the splendid love
Of that enchantress and the unearthly bliss
That in that oasis
Of dreams was his. Old was the man and weak.
And wearily the wreak

Of the hard years had worn the youth from him.
Deadening in heart and limb
The soul of fire that erst burnt fresh and high.
So, when the ecstasy,
Awhile by that infection of his quest
Kindled within his breast
Out of the embers of the ancient fire.
Grew cold, the feeble sire
In the full tide of bliss was like to drown.
The stressful glories strown
About his life did bum and weary him
Beyond his strength; his dim
And age-worn sense fail'd with the ecstasy;
And thus it came to be
That, in the gold and purple of the land,—
Midmost the arms that spann'd
Him round, the lips that on his lips still lay
And the deep orbs that aye
Flooded his spirit with their tireless light,—
Through all the dear delight
And glory of that life of flowers and dew,
Within the man there grew
A longing, half-unconsciously, to wear
Once more the weight of care
That deadens all the lives of mortal men,
A wish to feel again
The dull repose of the eventless days.
And from the stressful blaze
Of that too radiant dream once more to fade
Back to the level shade
Of thoughtless men's dull daily round of life.
Wherein there was no strife
Of earthly parts and forces to suffice
To joys of Paradise
Whose fire none scatheless save a god might know.
So day by day did grow
The longing, 'spite his wish, within his thought;
Albeit hard he fought
To conquer it, in all his looks it show'd;
And all that bright abode
Was grown to him like some fair hurtful fire
Of o'er-fulfill'd desire.
That eats the heart to madness. And one day,—
As on the breast he lay
Of that fair dame and in the radiant deep
Of her strange eyes did steep
His soul in burning languor,—it befell
That the unquellable

Desire burst up, no more to be reprèst,
Out of his weary breast
With a great bitter cry; and he was fain
To tell her of his pain
And of the mortal weakness, that in him
Stretch'd out—toward the rim
Of the sad world and the dull life-long bands—
Weary and weakling' hands
Of backward longing, being all too frail
And world-worn to avail
For the hot passionate splendour of the things
Of his imaginings.
"The dreams of youth come back to me too late,
Sweetheart," he said 'The gate
Of kindly death gapes wide for me; and I
Would fain go back to die
Among the towns and cities of my folk,
Under the wonted yoke
Of mortal custom; for I am but man.
Nor for all longing can
Shake off the leaden hand of age and use.
And now my limbs refuse
To bear the bliss of dreamland any more,
And all my soul is sore
With the long struggle. I had all forgot—
Whilst yet the flame was hot
Of the new-found delight—that I was old.
And that the creeping cold
Of death came very nigh upon my feet:
But now I feel it, sweet.
And may not tarry with thee any more,
That, with slow steps—before
The pale Archangel touch me—I again
May for awhile regain
The tents of men and die among my kin.
Repenting of my sin
And grasp for things beyond the reach or ken
Of miserable men.
Wherefore, I pray thee, kiss me yet once more—
For all my heart is sore
For parting from thee—and unspell my feet;
So haply I may greet
The dwellings of my kind before I die."
So he with many a sigh
Spake to the queen and told her all his mind.
And she,—that had divined
And known his yearning many a day and long.
Yet ever did prolong

The time of parting with the man,—with slow
Sad loving speech said, "Go:
I may not bid thee stay with me, poor friend.
That to the common end
Of weary men draw'st nigh, and (being man)
Labourest beneath the ban
Of the all-conquering pain and may'st not boar
The Miss thyself didst rear
In thy high fancy. Go: I love thee still,—
Better, perchance,—and fill
Thy destiny; for Fate is over all,
And one may not recall
The ordinance of God that fashion'd us.
Albeit despiteous
And very sad it seem." And kiss'd him thrice
Upon the brow, in guise
Of parting. Then the shape of her 'gan fade
Into the purple shade,
And all that dreamland melted into air.
And Ebhart,—standing there
Upon a desolate sweep of heathy plain,
Whereo'er the night did wane
And the June day came from the golden sills
Of heaven on the hills,—
Saw all the towers of gold and jasper fall
And knew beyond recall
His dream-built world with all its lovely might
Faded into the night;
And the hot tears brimm'd up his weary eyes.
Then close to him did rise
The carol of a lark; and it befell
That with the song the spell
Of grief was lightened, and some sadden'd peace
Came back to give him ease,
Upon that sunward hymning of the bird.
And looking round, he heard
A joyous neighing, and his true old steed
Came to him in his need
And rubb'd its head against his hand. So he
Mounted and o'er the lea
Rode, as the sun across the hills grew fair,—
And in the innocent air,
The flower-scents told pi the £Bur midmost June,
And the sweet early tune
Of the waked birds sang of the faded Spring
And the new flowering
Of the fresh fields with all the Summer weaves
Of bloom,—and in the sheaves

Of yellowing com, the sunlight lay like gold
Of consolation, told
By the dear God unto the earth rain-worn
And weary and betorn
With snow and tempest So the old squire rode
Upon the homeward road.
Among the fields, where all the world was glad
And none that he was sad
Had time to note,—and with the dying day
Came to a town, that lay
Childwise within the bosom of the hills.
And in the peace that fills
The hour of sunset, slept beneath the sky.
In one great panoply
Of crimson glory. And indeed it seem'd
Most like the thing he dream'd
Of the celestial city, where alone
This flesh shall have outgrown
The feebleness of life. And so he came
Into the town, all lame
And worn with travel and his hopes down cast;
And there he found at last
A little weary rest among strange men,
And was at peace again.
And there a resting-space he did abide;
And in the Autumn-tide
A little while thereafterward he died.

John Payne – A Concise Bibliography

The Masque of Shadows & Other Poems (1870)
Intaglios; Sonnets (1871)
Songs of Life and Death (1872)
Lautrec: A Poem (1878)
The Poems of François Villon (1878)
New Poems (1880)
The Book of the Thousand Nights and One Night (1882–4) A translation in nine volumes
Tales from the Arabic (1884)
The Novels of Matteo Bandello, Bishop of Agen (1890) A translation in six volumes
The Decameron by Giovanni Boccaccio (1886) A translation in three volumes
Alaeddin and the Enchanted Lamp; Zein Ul Asnam and The King of the Jinn: (1889) editor and translator
The Persian Letters of Montesquieu (1897) Translator
The Quatrains of Omar Kheyyam of Nisahpour (1898)
Poems of Master François Villon of Paris (1900)
The Poems of Hafiz (1901) A translation in three volumes
Oriental Tales: The Book of the Thousand Nights and One Night (1901) A translation in fifteen volumes

The Descent of the Dove & Other Poems (1902)
Poetical Works (1902) Two volumes
Stories of Boccaccio (1903)
Vigil and Vision: New Sonnets (1903)
Hamid the Luckless & Other Tales in Verse (1904)
Songs of Consolation: New Poems (1904)
Sir Winfrith & Other Poems (1905)
Selections from the Poetry of John Payne (1906) selected by Tracy and Lucy Robinson
Flowers of France: Romantic Period (1906)
Flowers of France, The Renaissance Period (1907)
The Quatrains of Ibn et Tefrid (1908, second edition 1921)
Flowers of France: The Latter Days (1913)
Flowers of France: The Classic Period (1914)
The Way of the Winepress (1920)
Nature and Her Lover (1922)
The Autobiography of John Payne of Villon Society Fame, Poet and Scholar (1926)

www.ingramcontent.com/pod-product-compliance
Lightning Source LLC
Chambersburg PA
CBHW060059050426
42448CB00011B/2529